WORLD'S MOST
DEADLY

—

By Karen McGhee

Australian
GEOGRAPHIC

WORLD'S MOST DEADLY

World's Most Deadly is published by Australian Geographic, an imprint of Bauer Media Ltd. All images and text are copyright © Bauer Media and may not be reproduced without the written permission of the publishers.

First published in 2016 by:

MEDIA GROUP

Bauer Media
54 Park Street, Sydney, NSW 2000
Telephone: (02) 9263 9813
Fax: (02) 9216 3731
Email: editorial@ausgeo.com.au

www.australiangeographic.com.au

Australian Geographic customer service:
1300 555 176 (local call rate within Australia).
From overseas +61 2 8667 5295

Editor Lauren Smith
Text Karen McGhee
Book design Brett Colbert
Art director Mike Ellott
Picture research Natsumi Penberthy
Print production Chris Clear
Sub-editor Natsumi Penberthy
Proofreader Ken Eastwood
CEO David Goodchild
Publishing Director – Specialist Division Cornelia Schulze
Publisher Jo Runciman
Editor-in-Chief, Australian Geographic Chrissie Goldrick

Printed in China by Leo Paper Products

RELATED TITLES:

Within the animal kingdom, there's no shortage of creatures that have evolved specialised bodies and techniques for killing their prey or defending their territory. Understanding and respecting these animals is the first and most important step in staying safe.

WORLD'S MOST
DEADLY

CONTENTS

ASIA
BENGAL TIGER

Most lists of the world's deadliest animals have the Bengal tiger close to the top. These big cats are thought to have killed more than 370,000 people in Asia during the 19th and 20th centuries.

Bengals are the second largest big cats living today and one of the five surviving tiger sub-species. Males can grow 3m long and weigh 300kg. They're big and powerful and also very territorial. They tend to

live and hunt in areas where humans like to set up villages, near grasslands at the edge of forests. This means tigers are more likely to come into contact with people than most other big cats.

LETHAL WEAPON

BITE

LETHAL WEAPON

CLAWS

FACT BOX

BITE OF STEEL

Tigers don't usually kill by ripping their prey apart. Instead, they lock their powerful jaws around their prey's neck and suffocate it to death.

Tigers usually prefer prey such as buffalo, wild boar and deer, but there are reports of rogue tigers that have become man-eaters. Among the most famous was the so-called Tigress of Champawat. She lived in Nepal during the 19th and early 20th centuries and became injured and unable to hunt her usual prey after being shot by a hunter. She turned to human prey and is said to have killed more than 400 people before eventually being killed.

TIGER SHARK

More than 450 species of shark have been identified, but only six have been known to attack humans. Of these, tiger sharks are one of the biggest repeat offenders. As of 2014, at least 31 people had been killed by tiger sharks worldwide in the past few hundred years.

A further 81 people have survived attacks. Tiger sharks are found in tropical coastal waters throughout Asia. Tiger shark jaws are so powerful and their serrated teeth so sharp that they can crack through the hard shells of marine turtles.

LETHAL WEAPON — BITE

SLOTH BEARS

Sloth bears might be mainly insect-eaters, but they react to predators with extreme aggression. They will attack anyone in their territory, particularly if they think their cubs are threatened. Sloth bears have long claws to help them break into termite mounds. They use these when they attack humans, typically striking at the face and head. Sloth bears live mostly alone in the forests of India, Sri Lanka, Bangladesh and Bhutan.

LETHAL WEAPON — CLAWS

LETHAL WEAPON — VENOM

FAT-TAILED SCORPIONS

The **venom** of fat-tailed scorpions is the most lethal of all scorpions. These eight-legged creatures are only about 10cm long, but the venom in their tail is such a powerful nerve poison it can kill a person in less than an hour. Each year, a few people are killed by fat-tailed scorpions, usually when they meet them in their natural habitat: the hot dry regions of India, northern Africa and the Middle East.

KING COBRA

A bite from this slithering reptile can bring down an elephant or kill a person within 30 minutes. Luckily, king cobras are as scared of people as we are of them and would prefer to use scare tactics before taking a bite. When threatened they'll rise up to the height of an adult person, with about a third of their body off the ground.

Then they'll flatten and flare out the skin around their head like a hood, hiss loudly and lunge forward as if they are going to strike. The king cobra's venom isn't quite as toxic as that of other deadly snakes, but it makes up for that by producing huge quantities of it. It's a mixture of deadly chemicals, but the main one is a powerful nerve poison called haditoxin. Victims experience excruciating pain, then become sleepy, dizzy and paralysed. The effects can be reversed with **antivenom**, often the same type developed to treat the bites of Australian tiger snakes. King cobras are found mostly in the forests of India, China, Malaysia, Indonesia and the Philippines.

LETHAL WEAPON

VENOM

FACT BOX

KING SIZED

The king cobra is the world's longest venomous snake. It can grow to a length of 5.5m.

LETHAL WEAPON
CLAWS

LETHAL WEAPON
VENOM

KOMODO DRAGON

Male Komodo dragons can grow to a length of more than 3m and a weight of about 160kg and they've got the jaws, teeth and claws you'd expect to see on a **voracious** meat-eater of this size. These massive reptiles are the world's biggest lizards and they normally prey on buffalos, wild pigs and deer, but they've also been known to attack humans. Fortunately people don't encounter them very often, as they're only found on Indonesia's remote Komodo Island and several smaller surrounding islands. The Komodo is an **ambush** hunter that launches surprise attacks on prey that passes too close; making short fast lunges while grabbing with its powerful claws and serrated shark-like teeth. It was discovered in 2009 that Komodo dragons also produce venom. This stops mammal blood from clotting so that even if prey manages to get away, it will ultimately bleed to death. The Komodo will track it patiently, waiting for it to bleed to death, then moving in for its meal.

FACT BOX

SUPER SENSE

Komodo dragons hear and see well, and have an exceptional sense of smell. They pick up odours by flicking out their forked tongues to 'taste' the air, like snakes do.

MOSQUITOES

These tiny insects are big killers – the world's biggest, in fact! Mosquitoes kill more people than any other animal; about one million people worldwide every year. What makes them so deadly are the infections they transfer into the bloodstreams of the victims they bite. Disease-causing mosquitoes thrive in the warm, wet conditions found throughout tropical Asia, where the main killer disease they carry is malaria. This is caused by a **parasitic microorganism** called plasmodium. Other potentially deadly human diseases passed on by mosquitoes in Asia include dengue fever, Japanese encephalitis and chikungunya. All are caused by viruses.

FACT BOX — LADY KILLERS

It's only female mosquitoes that bite – they need the protein in blood to produce eggs. Male mosquitoes feed on nectar, like butterflies do.

⚠ KEEP SAFE

The best form of protection against diseases mosquitoes can bring is to avoid getting bitten. The best way to do that, if you're in an area where mosquitoes carry viruses, is to cover up with light clothing and use a repellent that contains the chemical DEET. You can also speak with a doctor about preventive drugs or treatment.

LETHAL WEAPON
BITE

ASIATIC LION

The Asiatic lion is a subspecies of lion that's slightly smaller than its better-known African cousin. A formidable predator, it hunts in family groups and has killed humans. However, the Asiatic lion is now so endangered that humans are more of a threat to it than the other way round. The species used to live throughout Asia, but has been hunted so intensively that it's now classified as endangered, with only around 500 surviving in the wild.

LAST STAND

The remaining lions live in Gir Forest in India, where the population has been increasing since 2010.

BANDED KRAIT

These stunningly marked snakes are as dangerous as they are beautiful. Their venom is extremely toxic and potentially fatal to humans. The good news is that banded kraits aren't aggressive. In fact they're so docile that they're unlikely to attack a person, even when they're being hassled or provoked. If they do bite, a severe envenomation can lead to respiratory failure. They're found throughout South-East Asia.

SNAKE SNACK

The banded krait is known to feed mainly on other snakes, biting them and swallowing them headfirst.

LETHAL WEAPON
VENOM

WOLVERINE

There are good reasons why this creature has inspired aggressive comic book and movie characters. They are solitary hunters that are found across the northern parts of Europe, Asia and North America, near Arctic areas. Although they look like bears and grow as big as medium-sized dogs, they are relatives of weasels. What makes them such good hunters – and why we should stay clear of them – is that they're persistent, ferocious and incredibly strong for their size. They also have sharp claws and powerful jaws that can chomp through bone with ease. Wolverines eat a lot of smaller prey such as rabbits, but they'll also attack and bring down animals that are a lot bigger than them, such as reindeer.

FACT BOX

KEEP IT COOL

Wolverines have been known to stockpile their food for the future. They use the snow like a refrigerator, keeping their food fresh for times they aren't able to hunt.

LETHAL WEAPON

CLAWS

LETHAL WEAPON

BITE

POLAR BEAR

It doesn't take much for a polar bear to want to kill you. Just cross their path, and if they're hungry – which they usually are – you're not likely to survive. This is the world's largest land carnivore and it has no natural fear of people. Males reach an average weight of about 400kg and the length of a family car, and when they stand on their hind legs they can be more than 3m tall. Don't think that being big makes them slow – they can run as fast as Olympic sprinters. Because these bears usually live in isolated areas, humans don't often encounter them. But with their habitat now shrinking in size due to climate change, polar bears are increasingly wandering into towns around the Arctic circle looking for food.

LETHAL WEAPON
BITE

LETHAL WEAPON
CLAWS

POLAR PREY

Polar bears usually eat seals, which they stalk at the edge of the ice. They are also known to eat the carcasses of dead whales.

LETHAL WEAPON
VENOM

MEDITERRANEAN BLACK WIDOW SPIDER

This is Europe's most venomous spider. Its venom contains a potent nerve poison called latrotoxin. Symptoms after being bitten include sweating and muscle spasms. Victims can experience difficulty breathing, develop an irregular heart rate, vomit, or even die. Farm workers in the European grasslands are bitten most often.

FACT BOX   **LADIES ONLY**

Only the bite of the female Mediterranean black widow spider is dangerous to humans.

PORTUGUESE MAN O' WAR

The tentacles of the Portuguese man o'war are covered in stinging cells called **nematocysts**. These contain venom that stuns and kills prey that passes too close. Unfortunately, people swimming along Europe's coast during spring and summer are often stung. Occasionally the stings cause life-threatening allergic reactions, or can be so painful that they cause shock that leads to drowning.

LETHAL WEAPON
VENOM

BIG JOURNEY

Known in Australia as bluebottles, these floating creatures are blown all around the world, from Europe to the USA and down to the southern hemisphere.

EUROPE

ASP VIPER

Europe has fewer venomous snakes than any other continent bar Antarctica. There are a few species capable of killing people, and the asp viper is the most dangerous. Like other vipers it has large fangs that fold back when the mouth is closed. These are hollow and work like hypodermic syringes to inject venom into its victims. This makes the bite of the asp viper particularly painful. Despite the pain, most people will survive being bitten. However, every year a small percentage of victims die because they didn't receive medical treatment.

LETHAL WEAPON
VENOM

ANGRY AS AN ASP

They're usually slow-moving and timid snakes, but corner them and you'll see a very aggressive animal that will strike repeatedly.

EURASIAN WOLF

This is the big bad wolf you hear about in fairy stories, and there's lots of evidence from the past to show that wolves deserved their bad reputation. Historically, many people have been killed by wolves in Europe, particularly in France and eastern Europe. But it now seems that many of these attacks involved animals infected with rabies. This is a virus that affects the central nervous system. Wolves with the disease lose their fear of humans and become extremely aggressive. Rabies is now not nearly as common in Europe as it once was and so wolf attacks on humans are also a lot less common.

FACT BOX — PACK ATTACK

Wolves are extremely intelligent, and in the wild they live and hunt together in packs to bring down animals that are much larger than them, such as deer.

LETHAL WEAPON
BITE

ORCA

These supreme hunters of the sea are as fearsome as sharks, and maybe even a little more formidable because of their extraordinary intelligence. They have mouths full of 8cm-long teeth and big brains that enable them to communicate with each other so they can hunt together in packs. Orcas also have size and speed on their side. They grow to weights of more than five tonnes and are able to reach speeds of almost 50km/h. They live throughout the oceans of the world but are often seen in the icy waters off the United Kingdom and elsewhere in Europe. With a reputation as efficient hunters, the common name 'killer whale' seems fitting for orcas. Humans don't tend to swim in waters where orcas do, and aren't usually threatened by orcas, which would prefer to chase their usual prey of fish and seals. However, every so often, captive orcas have harmed or killed their human handlers.

FACT BOX
NUMBER ONE

The orca is the largest type of dolphin.

WILD BOAR

It's the tusks that make wild boar so dangerous. These are their incisor teeth, which grow particularly large and sharpen up as the males mature. Females have smaller sets. Mix these weapons with the aggressive territorial behaviour that many wild boar seem to have and you've got creatures that can rip you open if they think you're threatening them.

MIXING IT UP

Domesticated pigs were originally bred from wild boar. These days, boar also interbreed with farmyard pigs that have escaped into the wild.

Back off very quickly if you come across these animals in the European countryside.

AFRICA

NILE CROCODILE

You don't ever want to get close to the jaws of a Nile crocodile. They're weapons that bite down with a force more powerful than any other animal, and they're studded with dozens of razor-sharp teeth. If this animal got you in its mouth and the bite hadn't killed you, you'd drown anyway because they take all their prey underwater soon after they grab it. Every year, crocodiles claim the lives of several hundred people in Africa. These victims have usually made the mistake of wandering too close to the edges of rivers or lakes where crocodiles lurk motionless beneath the water.

LETHAL WEAPON

BITE

FACT BOX   **BAND AID**

The muscles that close a crocodile's jaws are incredibly powerful but the ones that open it aren't – so it's possible to hold the jaws of a Nile crocodile closed with just a rubber band!

BLACK MAMBA

This snake is one of the most feared animals in Africa, with a reputation for delivering the 'kiss of death'. No-one has been known to survive its highly toxic venom without treatment and each year it kills thousands of people across the continent. That's partly because the black mamba is widespread in Africa and people often come across it in remote areas. It doesn't help that it's also very aggressive and doesn't like to back down when confronted.

LETHAL WEAPON VENOM

SPEEDY SLITHERING

The black mamba is the fastest land snake in the world, able to move faster than most humans can run.

PUFF ADDER

No other snake causes as many deaths in Africa as this species. It occurs from about the middle of the continent down, and is often found living around villages and towns. It's an ambush predator that relies on camouflage to keep hidden while it waits for prey to pass by. Then it strikes with lightning speed. Usually, however, it's a slow-moving and bad-tempered reptile, and most of its victims stumble across it by accident. The good news is that its venom is slow-acting and with proper treatment almost 95 per cent of bite victims can be saved.

BIG KILLER

During the middle of last century, as many as 32,000 people a year died from puff adder bites in Africa.

EGYPTIAN COBRA

This species was worshipped by the ancient Egyptians. Its bite can kill a human in just 15 minutes and can bring down an adult elephant in three hours. The Egyptian cobra can be found living across northern Africa. Known also as the asp, it's the cobra species famed for its use in shows by African 'snake charmers'. Despite being one of the continent's most deadly snakes, this cobra is quite docile and will sometimes even 'play dead' when faced with a predator, such as a mongoose.

PHARAOH DEATH

It's thought that this is the species of snake that Cleopatra, a famous Egyptian pharaoh, used to commit suicide, because its venom works so quickly.

AFRICA

AFRICAN ELEPHANT

When you get in the way of the largest land animal on Earth and it's angry, you stand a very good chance of being crushed to death. Fully grown, African elephants weigh between two and six tonnes, and they can run at a top speed of about 25km/h, much faster than most humans can run.

FACT BOX

MORE MEETINGS

Deadly encounters between people and elephants are on the rise, as their habitat is destroyed.

LETHAL WEAPON

◄►

SIZE

SPOTTED HYENA

Hyenas have a reputation as scavengers but are among Africa's best hunters. They work together in packs, which can sometimes include as many as 70 hyenas. They're very good at chasing down large prey over distances, during which they can run for long periods of time at up to 60km/h. If you keep your distance, then they'll usually leave you alone.

PLAY MATES

Lions and hyenas often share territories, as they live in similar habitats, and will regularly squabble over fresh meat.

BLACK RHINOCEROS

Rhinos can reach weights of almost three tonnes, and have large horns at the front of their snouts. Combine these features with an ability to reach a speed of more than 60km/h if they decide to charge, and you'll want to keep well out of their way. On top of all this they've got poor eyesight and an unpredictable nature that makes them even more dangerous.

HUMAN HURT

Humans have hurt more rhinos than the other way round. Hunters have killed so many that this species is now critically endangered.

THE CAPE BUFFALO

The cape buffalo is a grazing **herbivore**, but it's aggressive. It's responsible for the deaths of about 200 hunters in Africa a year. Cape buffalo appear to be able to recognise and remember hunters who have previously tried to cause them or their herd harm. They've been known to ambush them and wound them when they return, even after many years.

WARNING SIGN

Cape buffalo will kill the cubs of adult lions that have been known to attack the herd, as a warning to not try it again.

HIPPOPOTAMUS

They might be vegetarians, but hippos cause more human deaths in Africa than any other large animal. According to some statistics, they kill almost 3000 people every year. They're actually highly aggressive creatures. The males are extremely territorial and will readily throw their bodyweight, which can be as much as 1.5 tonnes, around to keep anything and anybody away from their patch of riverbank. They also have huge jaws containing canine teeth that can be up to 50cm long. Female hippos are just as dangerous, because they're extremely protective of their young.

FACT BOX — CLASS TIME

A single male hippo will live with between five and 30 females and young. The collective noun for a group of hippos is a school!

AFRICAN LION

Lions are the only cats that live and hunt together in groups. It's a strategy that makes them extremely effective predators, able to bring down animals that are bigger and faster than they are. But lions will also kill much easier-to-catch creatures if they're about, and that includes humans. To lions, any humans in their habitats are seen as slow-moving, easy-to-catch prey – even inside reserves and safari parks.

LETHAL WEAPON
BITE

LETHAL WEAPON
CLAWS

LETHAL WEAPON
SIZE

FACT BOX — FAMILY FIGHT

Apart from crocodiles, the only large predators that will take on a male lion are other male lions.

⚠ KEEP SAFE

The same rule applies for lions as it does for human contact with all the big African animals – keep your distance and stay protected inside a car with the windows up.

DEATHSTALKER SCORPION

This deadly creature is found in the desert and dry scrublands of north-eastern Africa and has the most potent venom of any scorpion. An antivenom is available, but those who don't get it fast enough usually die. Deathstalkers are large as far as scorpions go, up to 11cm long. To avoid the heat and lack of water in their habitat they live in burrows by day and only emerge at night. They are ambush predators that hide under stones or bark and detect the vibrations of approaching prey. When prey passes, often spiders, centipedes or other scorpions, the deathstalker pounces and crushes it with its large pincers.

LETHAL WEAPON
VENOM

ACTUAL SIZE

FACT BOX — NEW USES

A substance called chlorotoxin, originally found in deathstalker venom, has been used to develop a new technology that's being trialled as part of a treatment for people with brain cancer.

TSETSE FLY

This blood-sucking insect looks very much like an ordinary housefly. But it's responsible for the debilitating and often fatal disease known as sleeping sickness, of which there are about 20,000 new cases in Africa every year. Victims inevitably die if they don't receive treatment for sleeping sickness. The disease is caused by a tiny single-celled parasite that's passed on by the tsetse fly, which it picks up from either a person or animal that's already infected.

FACT BOX — THE BIG SLEEP

About 65 million people in African countries south of the Sahara Desert are at risk of being infected with sleeping sickness through the bite of the tsetse.

LETHAL WEAPON
BITE

CHEETAH

Cheetahs are built for speed. Their lithe bodies are capable of reaching 70km/h for short bursts, which means they can take on the fastest animals in Africa. First, they stalk their prey to get as close as possible, staying downwind and hidden in tall grass. At the last possible moment, they leap out and attempt to knock it to the ground at high speed. They make their kill by locking their jaws around their prey's neck and suffocating it to death. Cheetahs can't roar like other big cats, but they're the only big cats that can purr.

A QUICK BITE

Because cheetahs are smaller than many of the big African carnivores, they need to eat their kills quickly or risk having them stolen by other predators.

AUSTRALIA

SALTWATER CROCODILE

Every year 4–10 people are attacked in Australia by saltwater crocodiles and usually one or two of them are never seen again. Salties live in northern Australia, in freshwater river systems and along coastlines. Their favourite attack zones are mangrove swamps and riverbanks and they can even be spotted swimming a long way out to sea. They breathe air, but have special adaptations that mean they can remain submerged for at least an hour, lurking silently just below the surface until they explode out and grab prey that comes too close.

Then they'll roll back in the water in a move known as a death roll. This either breaks their prey's neck or drowns it. If their prey is large they'll break it up into pieces and bury it in a kind of larder that they can come back to when they're hungry.

FACT BOX — BIG MOUTH

This is the world's biggest living reptile. Males can grow longer than 7m and weigh a tonne; about the size of the average family car.

LETHAL WEAPON

BITE

LETHAL WEAPON

CLAWS

SOUTHERN CASSOWARY

The southern cassowary is one of the world's most dangerous birds because of its size, reaching 1.8m, and territorial behaviour. They have a sharp, over-grown claw on the innerside of each foot. If they feel threatened they will kick out, and those razor-sharp claws could rip open a person like a switchblade.

PEACEFUL HOME

These tall, unpredictable birds live in rainforests in north-eastern Australia, where they mainly eat seeds.

BULL SHARK

This aggressive species of shark has powerful jaws and eats almost anything. It's the only shark that can handle freshwater for long periods, which means that it can leave the ocean and swim up freshwater river systems, where it's been known to take cattle, dogs and people.

SHALLOW SWIM

Bull sharks have even bitten and killed people wading or standing close to the shore.

SYDNEY FUNNEL-WEB

Sydney funnel-webs are among the scariest looking spiders, so it's fitting that they're also one of the world's deadliest. The females have black, hairy bodies that are up to 2.5cm long, although the more toxic males are slightly smaller. They put on a very fierce display when threatened. They rear up, lifting the body, front legs and huge fangs, and then thrust these down frighteningly fast. The fangs are each about 6mm long and capable of stabbing through a toenail. Even discounting the venom, these fangs hurt when they puncture skin!

LETHAL WEAPON

VENOM

ACTUAL SIZE

FACT BOX

SAFER DAYS

The highly toxic, fast-acting venom of the Sydney funnel-web killed at least 13 people between 1927 and 1980. Fortunately, no-one has died since an antivenom became available in 1981.

BOX JELLYFISH

There are lots of different box jellyfish around the world, and the marine creature with this name in Australia is one of the deadliest animals on the planet. Its sting can kill a healthy adult in minutes. Box jellyfish venom contains toxins that attack the nerves, blood and organs. It also contains 'dermatonecrotic' substances, which scar the skin. For that reason anyone lucky enough to survive an encounter with this creature will have lifelong scars. The box jellyfish has as many as 60 tentacles,

LETHAL WEAPON

VENOM

each up to 3m long. Venom is stored along these in millions of microscopic stinging cells called nematocysts. These each contain a tiny harpoon coiled inside that bursts out on contact to inject venom. Your chance of dying from a box jellyfish sting depends on the length of tentacles you come in contact with.

FLOATING KILLER

There have been 79 confirmed deaths in Australian waters caused by this predatory stinger since 1883.

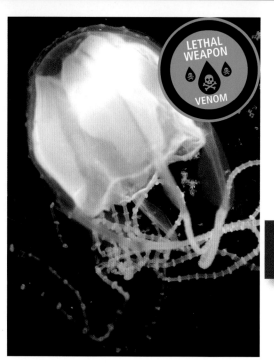

LETHAL WEAPON

VENOM

IRUKANDJI

Irukandji are a group of venomous jellyfish found in waters across northern Australia during summer. You don't always notice when you're stung, but later they cause one of nature's most awful experiences. It's called Irukandji syndrome and includes severe lower back pain and awful muscle cramps everywhere. There's sweating, anxiety, restlessness, nausea and vomiting. Headaches and heart palpitations develop, along with life-threatening high blood pressure and fluid build-up.

FACT BOX — MINI JELLIES

Most Irukandji have bodies that are no wider than 3cm, and thin wispy tentacles up to a metre long.

STINGERS

EASTERN BROWN SNAKE

This is Australia's most deadly snake. No other snake bites or kills more people in Australia than the eastern brown. It's about 1.5m long and has small fangs, but its venom packs more of a punch than most other snakes. It's ranked as the second-most toxic of any land snake in the world and has caused the deaths of at least 24 people since 1980. It usually claims one or two more victims every year. What makes this snake extra dangerous is its behaviour. It's fast-moving, aggressive, active during the day and found along the east coast, where most of Australia's population lives. All this means that it's also the snake most Aussies are likely to come in contact with, increasing the chances of being bitten.

MAIN MEALS

Eastern brown snakes mainly eat mammals, frogs, birds, reptiles and eggs.

LETHAL WEAPON
VENOM

BLUE-RINGED OCTOPUS

These are the world's most lethal octopuses. The venom in one sting is powerful enough to kill 26 adults. They've been responsible for two known deaths in Australia. These octopuses like to lurk in crevices in rock pools along the coast. They have fast-acting venom that can cause symptoms such as muscle weakness and paralysis within 10 minutes. Death can come in just 30 minutes. This usually results from a complete lack of oxygen to the brain due to breathing problems.

STAYING ALIVE

There's no antivenom available, but victims can survive if they are given CPR and placed on a respirator.

COASTAL TAIPAN

Before the introduction of an antivenom in 1956, taipan bites caused many deaths in Australia. The venom affects the blood and nervous system. It causes **nausea**, internal bleeding, muscle destruction and kidney damage. In severe cases, death can occur in just 30 minutes. It's an alert and nervous snake that does its best to stay out of the way of people, but if it's cornered it can be ferocious.

FACT BOX

SPECIAL SKILLS

Taipans have evolved so that their venom works especially well on warm-blooded animals.

GRIZZLY BEAR

All types of North American brown bear are called grizzlies. They're carnivores that will take large prey such as moose, elk and caribou if they can, but they also eat a lot of fish, fruits and berries. Each year, there's at least one or two fatal attacks on humans by grizzlies in North America. These usually occur when people have suddenly surprised a bear while they're walking in its territory. For this reason, making a lot of noise when you're in bear country is recommended so they know you're about. All encounters with grizzlies are potentially deadly, and running away once a bear is committed to an attack isn't an option because they can run at 60km/h. Mothers with cubs can be particularly aggressive and dangerous.

LETHAL WEAPON — BITE

LETHAL WEAPON — CLAWS

LETHAL WEAPON — SIZE

GRIZZLY GIANTS

Adult grizzly males can weigh more than 380kg, and can stand up to three metres tall when they're on their hind feet. Grizzly bears usually walk on all fours, but can rise up on two. It's usually a display of curiosity rather than aggression, but you wouldn't want to stick around to make sure!

AMERICAN ALLIGATOR

In the late 1960s, American alligator numbers dropped due to hunting and the destruction of wetlands to the point where they were dangerously close to extinction. Now, after more than 50 years, alligator numbers are back up and the species' survival seems to be assured. These carnivorous reptiles can reach huge proportions. Adult males can grow longer than 4m and reach a weight of about half a tonne.

Despite being often seen around human settlements, especially in Florida, there haven't been as many attacks as you'd expect. For example, from 1948 until mid-2006, just 17 people were confirmed killed by American alligators. In recent years, there has been a spate of attacks and it's believed that could be partly linked to the recovery of alligator numbers.

FACT BOX — LONG-LIVED

American alligators can live for up to 50 years in the wild. One of the reasons they live so long is that once they reach a length of over about one metre, they have no predators, except for humans.

LETHAL WEAPON — BITE

EASTERN DIAMONDBACK RATTLESNAKE

This is the biggest venomous snake in North America. It can reach a length of about 2.4m and a weight of about 4.5kg. Although it occasionally bites and kills people, the rattlesnake is not responsible for as many deaths as Hollywood movies suggest. Rattlesnakes prefer to keep their precious venom for prey and not waste it. That's what the rattles on the ends of their tails are for; to warn potential predators or large grazing animals that might step on them to stay away. Rattlesnake venom contains an extremely potent mix of toxins that attack the nervous system as well as blood and other tissues.

BLACK WIDOW SPIDER

The bite of the black widow is rarely fatal. It can, however, make people very sick with symptoms including aches, chills and fever, nausea and vomiting, severe stomach pains and extremely high blood pressure. Only female black widows bite, and only when they're disturbed while protecting their eggs.

OPEN WIDE

Rattlesnakes have big heads because they contain large venom glands. Around these are muscles that pump venom through their fangs and into their prey.

LETHAL WEAPON — VENOM

FACT BOX — EYE SPY

It's easy to identify a black widow by the red hourglass shape on its abdomen.

NORTH AMERICA

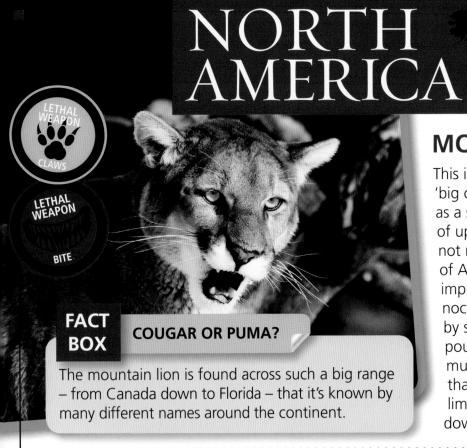

LETHAL WEAPON — CLAWS

LETHAL WEAPON — BITE

FACT BOX

COUGAR OR PUMA?

The mountain lion is found across such a big range – from Canada down to Florida – that it's known by many different names around the continent.

MOUNTAIN LION

This is North America's own version of a 'big cat', although technically it's classified as a small cat. Reaching a body length of up to 1.6m and a weight of 62kg, it's not nearly as big as the lions and tigers of Africa and Asia, though it is an equally impressive hunter. Mountain lions are nocturnal predators that hunt their prey by silently following and stalking it, then pouncing and grabbing at it with their muscular front legs, which are larger than their hind legs. These powerful limbs are specially adapted to bring down prey as large as elk or even moose.

BLACK BEAR

This is North America's most common bear species. Although black bears have attacked and killed people, they are not considered to be as much of a threat to people as the larger, more aggressive grizzlies. Black bears can be dangerous when they become used to finding their food near where humans congregate.

EASTERN CORAL SNAKE

The pattern of the eastern coral snake has come to be associated with such a toxic bite that other snakes have evolved to look like it as a form of protection from predators. Their venom contains potentially fatal **toxins**. There haven't been any human deaths from this snake since an antivenom was developed in the late 1960s.

COYOTE

People often hear the distinctive howl of coyotes, as they can be found living around cities, scavenging for food scraps. Attacks are rare, and they're not usually seen because coyotes are nocturnal and secretive. Away from human settlements, coyotes will usually hunt on their own or with a partner if they're after bigger prey.

EYES DOWN

Avoid making eye contact with bears as they will regard this as aggressive and see it as a challenge.

SLOW RELEASE

It can take more than 12 hours for a bite victim to feel the impact of the eastern coral snake's venom.

KEEP SWIMMING

Coyotes are very good swimmers – they've even managed to colonise islands in north-eastern USA.

FACT BOX — BIG FISH

Adult great whites usually grow to about 4.5m and weigh more than two tonnes. But records show that they can reach a length of 6m.

GREAT WHITE SHARK

The world's biggest predatory fish, the great white shark, is found in cooler waters on both sides of the North American continent. However, the threat they pose to people is surprisingly small. There's a far greater risk of being killed by bees or a lightning strike. Each year, on average, there are about 19 shark attacks in North American waters, including just one fatal attack every two years. Scientists believe most great white attacks are due simply to the animals being curious. The trouble is when you're as big as a great white with such huge jaws and multiple rows of sharp teeth, any bite can cause major, possibly fatal, injuries.

SOUTH AMERICA

JAGUAR

Jaguars kill their prey in a way that no other big cat does. Jaguars go for the head, biting directly through the skull to pierce the brain. It's a killing method that's highly effective, but can leave jaguars with broken teeth. These cats are stealth hunters that stalk their prey before suddenly bursting out from cover to kill it. Their spotted coats are great camouflage in the dense rainforests of South and Central America, where they roam. It makes it almost impossible for prey to see jaguars until it's too late.

LETHAL WEAPON
BITE

FACT BOX — WET OR DRY

Most cats hate water and prefer to stay away from rivers and streams, but not jaguars. They're excellent swimmers and find a lot of their prey in and around water, including turtles and caiman – a type of crocodile.

POISON DART FROG

There are more than 100 different species of poison dart frog in Central and South America. Most are brightly coloured and for good reason. The stunning blue, red and yellow hues of their skin warn that they are **poisonous** and best avoided. Native South Americans have been using this to their advantage for hundreds of years, by dipping their hunting darts in toxic secretions from the glands on the backs of these frogs.

FACT BOX — POTENTIAL PREDATORS

When poison dart frogs are raised in captivity they don't always have the poisons, unless they are fed on the same creatures that they eat in the wild.

LETHAL WEAPON
ELECTRIC SHOCK

GOING MISSING

People sometimes disappear from the Amazon or Orinoco rivers, and it's thought that some may have drowned after receiving an electric shock.

ELECTRIC EEL

This freshwater fish can produce large amounts of electricity, which it uses to stun prey, as protection from predators and to communicate with other electric eels. They are able to produce electrical bursts of up to 600 volts, which is enough to stun or even kill an adult human. These fish produce electricity using three special electric organs. Inside these are thousands of specialised cells called electrocytes that function like tiny batteries.

PIRANHA

Piranha are **carnivorous** freshwater fish famed for their razor-sharp teeth and aggressive attitude. They're also known for working together in a frenzied group to bring down prey that's considerably bigger than they are, which includes people who make the mistake of swimming in piranha-infested waters. There are about 30 different species of piranha and all of them are found naturally only in the lakes and rivers of South America. Most are carnivores, but a few are vegetarians. Recent research shows that the reason they school in groups probably has a lot do with them using the safety-in-numbers approach to protect themselves from predators, such as bigger fish. They do act as a group to attack large mammals, including humans, but those mammals are usually weakened or injured in some way first.

RARE OFFENDERS

Although people have died from piranha attacks in the Amazon River, fatalities are extremely rare.

LETHAL
WEAPON
BITE

OUT OF RANGE

Sadly, in 2013, in the Canadian province of New Brunswick, two young boys, aged 5 and 7, were crushed to death by a green anaconda while they were sleeping in an apartment over a pet shop from where the snake had escaped.

LETHAL WEAPON — SIZE

GREEN ANACONDA

Able to grow longer than 8m and attain a weight of almost 30kg, South America's green anaconda is the world's biggest snake. Although southeast Asia's reticulated python can reach a slightly longer length, no snake is heavier. The green anaconda is non-venomous and semi-aquatic. It hunts in murky swamps and streams. With its nostrils and eyes positioned on top of its head it is able to lurk silently and mostly submerged, waiting for prey to come and take a drink. Then it grabs it with its teeth and coils its long muscular body around it, eventually crushing and suffocating it to death, before swallowing it whole. Adult green anaconda prey on large mammals such as wild pigs, tapirs and capybaras. They may also prey on people, although they're not often encountered in green anaconda habitat.

SOUTH AMERICAN RATTLESNAKE

The bite of this snake is potentially deadly, and if it doesn't kill you it can cause permanent disabilities. It's found mostly in dry or arid habitats. It usually preys on mammals, although it will sometimes catch and eat lizards. South American rattlesnake venom contains potent nerve poisons that can cause a victim to become progressively **paralysed**. This effect can be so strong that the neck becomes limp and appears to be broken, which can make breathing difficult and ultimately impossible without medical help. Blindness, which can often be permanent, is another nasty symptom.

WIDESPREAD

This snake has the largest range of any rattlesnake, covering all of mainland South America, except Chile and Ecuador.

THE GOLDEN LANCEHEAD

This tree-climbing snake is found only on one tiny island off the coast of Brazil, Queimada Grande. It's a type of snake known as a pit viper; a group that contains the dreaded rattlesnakes. What sets pit vipers apart from other snakes is that they have special pits on their heads, between the eyes and the nostrils, that detect heat. These heat-detecting organs can sense infrared radiation, which means they can detect the warmth given off by the bodies of their prey. They can do this from up to a metre away. It's like being able to see in the dark.

MAIN MEAL

This snake likes to eat birds and mammals, but will take lizards if they come too close.

BRAZILIAN WANDERING SPIDERS

These spiders are aggressive, very deadly and big. There are eight different species of Brazilian wandering spiders and some have a leg span of more than 15cm! These spiders are found in jungle habitats where they hide during the day under rocks or logs, in plants or inside termite mounds. At night they come out to wander across the forest floor looking for prey.

Brazilian wandering spider venom contains a nerve poison and although the killing power of the species varies, these are generally considered to be the world's most venomous spiders.

FACT BOX

NAME SAKE

The scientific name for these spiders – *Phoneutria* – means 'murderess'.

ACTUAL SIZE

Glossary

ambush	To hide and wait quietly then make a surprise attack.
antivenom	Medicine for people who have been bitten by venomous animals.
carnivorous	Describes an animal that eats meat.
herbivore	An animal that eats only plants.
nausea	The sick feeling when you want to vomit.
nematocysts	Specialised cells in jellyfish, or their relatives, that contain a barbed sting with venom.
paralysed	Unable to feel or move.
parasitic	Describes a plant or animal that lives on or in another plant or animal.
poisonous	Full of, containing or producing a toxin that is harmful.
microorganism	An animal or plant so small that you need a microscope to see it.
toxin	A poison produced by a plant or animal.
venom	A poison that an animal produces and injects into another animal.
voracious	Having a big appetite and eating a large quantity of food.

FURTHER READING

World's Most Endangered
2015, Australian Geographic

World's Most Dangerous Animals
2012, Animal Planet

The Concise Animal Encyclopedia
2013, Australian Geographic

Children's Animal Atlas
2015, Australian Geographic

PHOTOGRAPHER AND ILLUSTRATOR CREDITS
Listed by page, clockwise from top left.

Front Cover: Danita Delimont/Getty; Tim Flach/Getty; Filip Fuxa/Getty; Dirck Ercken/Shutterstock (SS); Donovan van Staden/SS; Anton Ivanov/SS; Yusran Abdul Rahman/SS; Ends: ZoneFatal/SS; Page 1: Dennis W. Donohue/SS; Page 3: Eric Isselee/SS; Dsanimal/SS; Page 4: Piyaphon/SS; Page 5: James Warwick/Getty; AndreAnita/SS; Page 6: Marjorie Crosby-Fairall/Australian Geographic (AG); Dennis W. Donohue/SS; Nagel Photography/SS; Page 7: Thomas Marent/Getty; Benzine/SS; Page 8: Pius Lee/SS; Gudkov Andrey/SS; Page 9: Kletr/SS; DEA / DANI-JESKE/Getty; Photocech/SS; Page 10: Michal Ninger/SS; Page 11: Andy Rouse/Getty; Sciencepics/SS; Matteo photos/SS; Page 12: Matteo photos/SS; Roger Eritja/Getty; Page 13: Morales/Getty; Vladyslav Danilin/SS; Page 14: Jason Edwards/Getty; Johan Swanepoel/SS; Page 15: reptiles4all/SS; Eric Esselee/SS; Stuart G Porter/SS; Page 16: JMx Images/SS; Mogens Trolle/SS; Gerrit de Vries/SS; Peter Schwarz/SS; Page 17: Anton Ivanov/SS; Dennis Jacobsen/SS; Page 18: ANP/SS; Ivanov Gleb/SS; Page 19: Imagemore Co Ltd/Getty; Maggy Meyer/SS; Martin Dohrn/SPL/Getty; Page 20: David Hancock/AG; Kristian Bell/SS; Danikancil/Getty; Marek Velechovsky/SS; Page 21:Esther Beaton/AG; Esther Beaton/AG; Page 22: Nick Rains/AG; Johan Larson/SS; Lisa-Ann Gershwin/AFP/Getty; Page 23: Kristian Bell/SS; reptiles4all/SS; Chanwit Polpakdee; Page 24: Critterbiz/SS; Page 25: Eric Isselee/SS; Meister Photos/SS; Jim Merli/Getty; Page 26: Scott E. Read/SS; Brenda Carson/SS; Patrick K. Campbell/SS; Josef Pittner/SS; Page 27: Stuart Westmorland/Getty; Stefan Pircher/SS; Page 28: Mikadun/SS; Cuson/SS; Erik Isselee/SS; Page 29: Luca Gavagna/Getty; Risteski Goce/SS; Page 30: Vladimir Wrangel/SS; David Persson/SS; Page 31: Eric Isselee/SS; Maria Maarbes/SS; Dr. Morley Read/SS; Page 32: Dennis W. Donohue/SS; Back Cover: sciencepics/SS; Michael Duva/Getty; Rolf E. Staerk/SS; Andrew Burgess/SS; AMST/SS; reptiles4all/SS

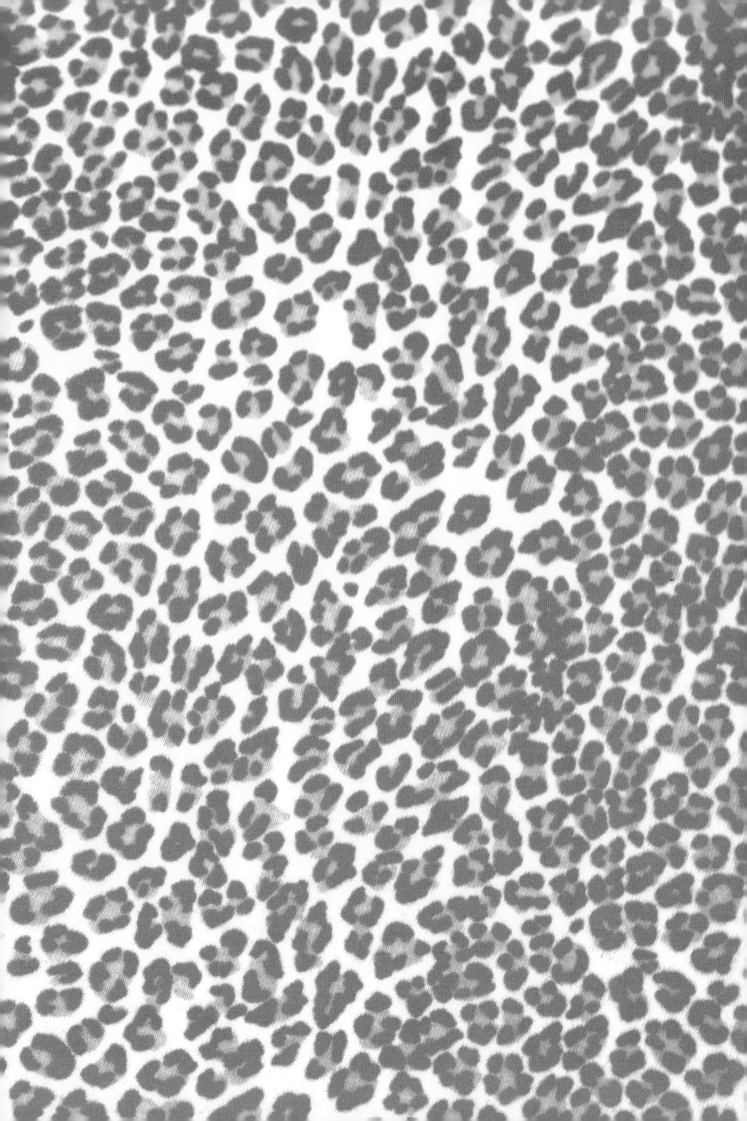

Komodo dragon

WORLD'S MOST
DEADLY

Portuguese man o' war

LETHAL WEAPON
BITE

If you go down to the woods today, you're in for a big surprise! So stay in and read about the nasties you'll find there: from North America's grizzly bears to Europe's wolves.
In Africa, stay clear of the black mamba's 'kiss of death', and in South America's rainforests keep out of the path of the Brazilian wandering spider.
It's no safer downunder in Australia, where huge saltwater crocs lurk just beneath the water, or in Asia, where you need to watch out for big cats!

By Karen McGhee

Mosquito ▲

King cobra

Piranha

African lion

ISBN-13: 978-1742458014

9 781742 458014